Widow Clicquot

The True Story of the Champagne Woman

Harper Blackwood

Copyright

Disclaimer

The information offered in *Widow Clicquot: The True Story of the Champagne Woman* is based on considerable research, historical records, and published literature about Barbe-Nicole Clicquot Ponsardin and the champagne industry at the time. While every attempt has been taken to assure the information's correctness, some details and interpretations are limited by historical evidence and the author's perspective.

This book is designed solely for informational and educational purposes, and should not be regarded as a complete or exhaustive explanation of the subject. To create a more compelling narrative, the author has interpreted certain events, discussions, and personal experiences creatively. Any resemblance to actual persons, alive or dead, other than those explicitly recognized, is entirely coincidental.

The author and publisher make no guarantees or warranties on the correctness, applicability, or completeness of the contents of this book. The reader is invited to conduct their own research and consult additional sources to gain a more thorough grasp of the issues covered.

Neither the author nor the publisher will be held liable for any damages, losses, or other liabilities resulting from the use or misuse of the material in this book. All brand names, trademarks, and registered trademarks referenced within are the property of their respective owners and are used solely for reference reasons.

Table of Contents

Introduction

In the early nineteenth century, when women were mostly restricted to the home, one woman dared to challenge convention and alter an industry. Barbe-Nicole Clicquot Ponsardin, also known as the Widow Clicquot, was more than just a champagne pioneer; she was a visionary leader who revolutionized the commercial landscape, creating an enduring legacy that continues to resonate today. Her narrative is one of extraordinary courage, innovation, and tenacity, set in post-revolutionary France, a moment of enormous upheaval and potential.

Widowed at the age of 27, Barbe-Nicole faced a difficult decision: sell her late husband's struggling wine business or assume the reins alone in a male-dominated industry that was everything but hospitable to women. Choosing the latter, she went on a journey that would take her through enormous hurdles, ranging from the Napoleonic Wars to the complexities of Champagne production. She not only salvaged the company but also took it to new heights thanks to her tenacity and unwavering pursuit of greatness.

Widow Clicquot: The True Story of the Champagne Woman dives into the life and legacy of this remarkable woman. It reveals the technologies she pioneered that transformed champagne production, the strategic decisions that guaranteed her brand's global position, and the personal sacrifices she made along the way. This book is more than a biography; it is a monument to a trailblazer whose impact goes far beyond Champagne's vineyards.

As you turn the pages, you'll meet the lady behind the distinctive yellow label—her difficulties, successes, and the unwavering attitude that made her a legend. Whether you are a champagne aficionado, a history buff, or someone looking for inspiration from a well-lived life, this book provides a captivating portrait of Barbe-Nicole Clicquot Ponsardin, sometimes known as the Grand Dame of Champagne.

Chapter One

The Early Life of Barbe-Nicole

Barbe-Nicole Ponsardin, the famed Widow Clicquot, was born on December 16, 1777, in the bustling city of Reims, France. Her biography is one of tenacity, intelligence, and determination, qualities that would later distinguish her as a champagne industry pioneer. However, before becoming a strong entrepreneur, Barbe-Nicole was a little girl growing up in a society marked by political upheaval, sociological change, and the limits placed on women in the 18th century.

Reims, a city rich in history and tradition, was the center of the French champagne region. It was a region where vineyards stretched across the undulating hills, and winemaking was profoundly ingrained in the culture. Barbe-Nicole was born into the wealthy and influential Ponsardin family, which was well-known in the city's social and political circles. Her father, Nicolas Ponsardin, was a successful textile dealer who eventually became a magistrate. Her mother, Jeanne Josephe Marie-Clémentine Letertre-Huart, was from an equally illustrious family. Together, they gave Barbe-Nicole a privileged upbringing that would prepare her for the difficult world she would later face.

Barbe-Nicole was exposed to the complexities of business and social etiquette from an early age. Her father, a savvy businessman, frequently engaged her in discussions about commerce and trade. Unlike many other girls her age,

Barbe-Nicole was encouraged to think critically and join in discussions about business, politics, and society. This early exposure to the corporate world would come in handy later in life, when she took over the family business.

The Ponsardins were fervent Catholics, and religion played an important role in Barbe-Nicole's childhood. She was schooled at a convent, where she learned religious subjects, reading, writing, and math. The monastery also taught young girls the values of modesty, obedience, and piety, all of which were highly esteemed among women at the time. However, Barbe-Nicole's education was not limited to household skills. Her father made sure she was well-versed in the larger world, teaching her the value of tenacity, ingenuity, and adaptability to changing situations.

As Barbe-Nicole got older, France's political scene saw tremendous changes. The French Revolution, which began in 1789, was a period of intense instability and uncertainty. The revolution resulted in the overthrow of the monarchy, the creation of extreme political groupings, and severe social unrest. For the Ponsardin family, the revolution represented both terror and opportunity. While many aristocratic families experienced persecution, the Ponsardins were able to negotiate the dangerous political waters, thanks in large part to Nicolas Ponsardin's ability to integrate with the new political order.

Despite the obstacles of the revolution, Barbe-Nicole's family thrived. Her father's business savvy meant that they retained their money and prestige even as their surroundings altered. Barbe-Nicole acquired some of her most significant life lessons during this time of turmoil, including the value of flexibility, the significance of strategic relationships, and the strength of tenacity.

Barbe-Nicole married François Clicquot, the wealthy and influential wine merchant's son, when she was 21 years old. The marriage was arranged, as is common for families of their status, but it was also a match founded on mutual respect and aspiration. François was enthusiastic about the wine business and had ambitious intentions to grow the Clicquot family's operations. Barbe-Nicole, with her smart mind and great financial sense, immediately became his confidante and collaborator in these ventures.

Barbe-Nicole and François went on a journey to establish a profitable wine business. However, their partnership was cut short when François died unexpectedly in 1805, leaving Barbe-Nicole as a widow at the age of 27. This heartbreaking loss triggered a turning point in her life. Barbe-Nicole bucked cultural norms during a time when widows were expected to withdraw from public life and mourn in silence. Instead of withdrawing, she decided to take over the family business, determined to realize the goal she and François had shared.

Barbe-Nicole's move to take control of the company was brave and unprecedented. Women, particularly widows, were viewed as incapable of running sophisticated businesses, particularly one as demanding as winemaking. But Barbe-Nicole was undeterred. Drawing on her father's lessons and the experiences she shared with François, she began to negotiate the male-dominated world of wine production and trading.

The early years presented numerous problems. The wine business was still recovering from the effects of the Napoleonic Wars, and the economic situation was unstable. Barbe-Nicole encountered mistrust from her classmates and opposition from those who questioned her talents. Despite this, she persisted, steering the company through these trying times with her acute intelligence, business savvy, and thorough mastery of the art.

Chapter Two

The Birth of the Champagne Industry

The history of champagne is as effervescent as the drink itself, with tales of creativity, resilience, and an unwavering pursuit of perfection. Long before Barbe-Nicole Clicquot made an indelible stamp on the business, the world of champagne was a much different place—one laden with problems, potential, and the beginnings of what would become one of history's most renowned beverages.

Champagne was still in the process of defining itself in the late 18th century. Champagne, located in northeastern France, had long been a viticultural hotspot, but the sparkling wine we know today was not yet well established. The winemakers of the time produced still wines, which were frequently crimson and very different from what we now know with the term "champagne." The wine-making process was tedious and unpredictable, and the chilly environment of the region frequently resulted in an unintentional second fermentation in the bottles during the spring. This secondary fermentation was initially regarded as a flaw—a problem to be resolved rather than a feature to be embraced.

The bubbling wine, with its effervescence and lightness, grew in popularity, but it remained a specialist product. In truth, the early days of sparkling wine were fraught with obstacles. Bottles would frequently explode due to the pressure of carbon dioxide produced during the second fermentation, earning them the nickname "devil's wine." The corks available at the time were insufficient to withstand the pressure, and glass technology had not advanced to the point where bottles could consistently hold the bubbling wine. This made champagne manufacturing both dangerous and expensive, and many winemakers were unwilling to fully embrace this explosive beverage.

However, the attractiveness of the bubbles began to pique the interest of a select few. Among them were monks from the Abbey of Hautvillers, who were experimenting with techniques to control and harness the secondary fermentation. According to legend, Dom Pierre Pérignon, a Benedictine monk from Hautvillers, was one among the early pioneers who worked ceaselessly to perfect the process. Dom Pérignon is widely mythologized as the originator of champagne, but his genuine contribution was to improve the quality of wine produced in the Champagne region. He concentrated on mixing different varietals to make a more balanced and pleasant wine, as well as developing procedures to strengthen bottles and enhance the corking process. These advances, while significant, were merely the start of the trip.

Barbe-Nicole Clicquot entered the champagne industry at a critical juncture. The French Revolution upended France's social and economic systems, including the wine business. Many vineyards and wineries were confiscated, sold, or abandoned during this turbulent time. However, the demise of the old system created new chances. The increasing middle class, together with the ascent of Napoleon Bonaparte, rekindled interest in luxury items, notably champagne. As the French troops marched across Europe, so did the demand for French wines, creating new markets and opportunities for entrepreneurial winemakers.

In this setting, Barbe-Nicole married François Clicquot, the son of a wealthy wine trader. The Clicquot family had been in the wine business for several generations, but it was François who first saw the value of focusing on champagne. Following their marriage, François and Barbe-Nicole collaborated to grow the family business, but their efforts were met with minimal success. François was a visionary, but he lacked the business acumen and health to fully actualize his ambitions. Barbe-Nicole was 27 years old when her husband died in 1805, leaving her a widow with a young daughter and a difficult business to run.

Barbe-Nicole faced a difficult decision following her husband's death: sell the firm and retire to a quiet life, or take over and continue her husband's job. Despite the enormous hurdles ahead, she chose the latter, becoming one of the first women in history to run a champagne house. At the time, it was almost unheard of for a woman to run a business, let alone one in the fiercely competitive and male-dominated wine sector. Barbe-Nicole remained unfazed. She recognized champagne's potential as a symbol of celebration, luxury, and sophistication, rather than merely a product.

Under her direction, the Veuve Clicquot (or "Widow Clicquot") brand began to emerge. She recognized that in order to succeed, she needed to set her champagne apart from the competition. One of her most notable accomplishments was the creation of the riddling process, which enabled the manufacturing of clear, sediment-free champagne. Before this discovery, champagne was frequently hazy and unattractive to the eye. Barbe-Nicole's method entailed positioning the bottles at an angle and gradually turning them so that the sediment settled in the bottle's neck. This sediment could then be easily removed, yielding a clear, sparkling wine. The riddling table, as it became known, revolutionized champagne production and established a quality standard that is still in use today.

Barbe-Nicole was also a savvy marketer. She realized the value of branding and was among the first to recognize the significance of the bottle label. She made sure that each bottle of Veuve Clicquot had the unique yellow label that is still used today. This label not only set her champagne apart from competitors, but it also became a symbol of quality and status. Her branding efforts extended beyond the label; she assiduously controlled Veuve Clicquot's image as a luxury product, linking it with monarchy, nobility, and the social elite.

As Napoleon's wars spread over Europe, so did the popularity of Veuve Clicquot. Barbe-Nicole profited on the European aristocracy's need for luxury goods, exporting her champagne to Russia, England, and beyond. Her champagne became the drink of choice for celebrations and special events, establishing its place in Europe's cultural heritage. The Russian market, in particular, became a significant source of revenue for the Clicquot brand. The Russian aristocracy adored the light, effervescent drink, which they affectionately dubbed "the widow's wine." However, this triumph did not come without hurdles. The Napoleonic Wars disrupted trade channels, making it difficult to keep supply steady. However, Barbe-Nicole's persistence and resourcefulness enabled her to overcome these challenges and continue to expand her firm.

Barbe-Nicole's tale is more than just one of commercial success; it also demonstrates her tenacity in the face of hardship. She suffered personal grief, cultural expectations, and the constant fear of failure, yet she persevered. Her capacity to adapt, develop, and lead with a clear vision distinguished her from her peers, laying the groundwork for what would become one of the most successful champagne companies in history.

The birth of the champagne industry, as we know it, is intrinsically related to Barbe-Nicole Clicquot's life and career. Her contributions to the industry were both technical and cultural. She elevated champagne from a regional curiosity to a global symbol of celebration. Her legacy lives on in every bottle of Veuve

Clicquot, a brand that still represents the same principles of quality, innovation, and elegance that she advocated for almost two centuries ago.

The actual story of the Champagne Woman depicts not just the birth of an industry, but also the indomitable spirit of a woman who refused to be bound by the constraints of her time. Barbe-Nicole Clicquot's rise from widow to wine magnate is a tale of bravery, inventiveness, and the unwavering pursuit of success. It's a story that continues to inspire and resound, much like the bubbles in a glass of her best champagne.

Chapter Three

The Widow Takes Over

Barbe-Nicole Ponsardin, a young woman born into a life of affluence, reached a watershed moment in her life in 1805 when her husband, François Clicquot, died. Barbe-Nicole became a widow at the age of 27, which was more than a personal tragedy in the early nineteenth century. It was a sociological and economic barrier, particularly in a male-dominated culture where women were rarely assigned corporate duties.

François was a visionary, seeing possibilities in the sparkling wine sector long before it was recognized and distinguished. However, his sudden demise placed his fledgling champagne business in jeopardy. The Clicquot family, who had already invested considerably in the company, was presented with a difficult decision: sell it or keep it operating. Barbe-Nicole made a daring and uncommon move at an era when women were expected to retire to a life of mourning and solitude following the deaths of their husbands: she elected to take over the business herself.

This decision was not without risk. The wine industry was unpredictable, necessitating a precise balance of agricultural, scientific, and business skills. Furthermore, France's political and economic landscape at the period was volatile, with the Napoleonic Wars adding to the instability. Nonetheless, Barbe-Nicole's resolve was unwavering. She was not willing to let her husband's dreams perish alongside him. Instead, she would go ahead, motivated by her trust in the company's potential and a desire to honor François' legacy.

Barbe-Nicole's first issue was taking control of the company. Despite marrying into the Clicquot family, she was not immediately recognized as the company's head. In fact, the Clicquots were originally apprehensive to let her lead. The concept of a woman running a business, especially one as intricate as a champagne house, was unthinkable. Women were frequently perceived as lacking the requisite skills to negotiate the world of industry, and many people predicted that the company would collapse under her leadership.

Barbe-Nicole, on the other hand, refused to give up. She utilized her wit, charm, and unwavering determination to persuade her father-in-law, Philippe Clicquot-Muiron, to give her a chance. She claimed that her intimate knowledge of her husband's goals and expertise of the business made her the best option to head it. Philippe reluctantly consented, but with one condition: she had just a few years to prove herself. If the company wasn't profitable by then, it would be sold.

With this conditional license, Barbe-Nicole set out on a journey that would shape her life and alter the champagne business. She was fully aware that the odds were stacked against her. She had to learn rapidly, understanding the delicate mechanics of champagne production, from grape cultivation to fermentation, all while managing the company's finances and navigating a difficult political situation.

One of Barbe-Nicole's initial strategic decisions was to surround herself with skilled consultants. She sought out professionals in viticulture and winemaking, knowing that their knowledge would be critical to her success. Among them was Antoine de Muller, the cellar master who would become one of her most dependable allies. Together, they experimented with several production processes in order to increase champagne quality and streamline the manufacturing process. Barbe-Nicole's willingness to innovate would become one of her distinguishing characteristics, separating her from her competition.

Her first big accomplishment came with the invention of the "riddling" technique, which entailed placing the bottles at an angle and spinning them frequently to accumulate sediment in the neck, which could then be readily removed. This approach greatly increased the champagne's clarity and quality, making it more desirable to customers. The invention of the riddling table was revolutionary, and it is still used in champagne production today. This innovation not only improved the product, but also revealed Barbe-Nicole's dedication to perfection, bolstering her industry standing.

Despite her early triumphs, Barbe-Nicole had significant hurdles. The political instability created by the Napoleonic Wars hindered trade channels, making it impossible to export champagne. The British embargo of continental Europe, in particular, severely restricted her access to the lucrative Russian market, where champagne was highly sought after by the elite. Undeterred, Barbe-Nicole discovered innovative solutions to overcome these limitations. She worked tirelessly to establish relationships with her clientele, ensuring that her champagne reached them despite the obstacles provided by the war.

Barbe-Nicole's determination paid off when, in 1814, she made a risky move that irrevocably altered the trajectory of her business. With the war nearing its end, she placed her whole output on a single shipment of champagne to Russia, hoping that the Russian elite, celebrating Napoleon's defeat, would be ready to partake in the luxurious drink. Her gamble paid out spectacularly. The supply arrived in time for the festivities, and the Russian market's reaction was enormous. The demand for Veuve Clicquot champagne surged, and Barbe-Nicole's name became synonymous with luxury and prestige.

This victory not only saved her business, but also cemented Veuve Clicquot's position as one of the world's premier champagne houses. Barbe-Nicole's ability to manage the complexities of international trade, combined with her unique approach to production, distinguished her from her competitors. She had demonstrated that she was more than capable of directing the company, and she had done so in a way that defied expectations at the time.

Barbe-Nicole's business expanded, and she continued to develop. She introduced the first known vintage champagne in 1810, which involves making champagne from grapes picked in a single year rather than combining wines from numerous years. This enabled her to design a product that was both distinctive and consistently good in quality, thereby improving her brand's reputation. She also placed a strong emphasis on branding, realizing the value of building a distinctive and respectable image for her champagne. Veuve Clicquot's characteristic yellow label, added later in the nineteenth century, became one of the wine industry's most famous trademarks.

Barbe-Nicole's success as an entrepreneur was even more impressive given the societal restraints of her day. As a widow, she was expected to live a quiet life of sorrow, but she opted to defy expectations and carve out a place for herself in the business world. Her leadership style was a mix of practicality and inventiveness, and she was not hesitant to take chances to attain her objectives. Her narrative is one of persistence, determination, and unflinching faith in her own potential to succeed.

Widow Clicquot's legacy is not only that of a great business, but also of a woman who changed women's roles in business. She demonstrated that gender was not a barrier to success, and that with vision, determination, and a willingness to create, anything was achievable. Her tale continues to inspire entrepreneurs and business leaders all across the world, serving as a reminder that people who challenge convention frequently achieve great success.

Barbe-Nicole's transformation from a young widow facing an uncertain future to a trailblazing businesswoman demonstrates her strength of character and imaginative approach to business. She changed the champagne industry and created a brand that is still thriving more than two centuries later. Her narrative is not just about a great woman, but it also reflects the possibilities that occur when one has the fortitude to take control of one's fate, even in the face of insurmountable difficulties. Every glass of Veuve Clicquot champagne contains the spirit of Widow Clicquot—a history of creativity, excellence, and unwavering determination.

Chapter Four

Innovation and Growth

Barbe-Nicole Clocquot Ponsardin, better known as the Widow Clicquot, was a woman who not only defied societal standards but also altered the champagne business with her revolutionary spirit. She broke down boundaries during a time when women were mostly confined to household tasks, becoming a strong force in a male-dominated economic world. Her narrative of invention and success is about more than just expanding a business; it is about visionary concepts that would permanently impact the manufacture and image of Champagne.

Barbe-Nicole was at a crossroads after her husband, François Clicquot, died unexpectedly.

The easy option would have been to sell the family business and live the tranquil life expected of a widow in early nineteenth-century France. However, she chose the route of resilience and tenacity, which resulted in one of the most significant champagne developments in history. Her choice to continue her husband's job was motivated by more than simply a sense of duty; it was powered by a love of the winemaking trade and a strong belief in champagne's potential.

Barbe-Nicole's success was built on a constant quest of perfection. She recognized that in order to set her champagne apart from the many others on the market, she needed to innovate. The first important breakthrough under her supervision was the production of the first vintage champagne. Until then, champagne was often a combination of wines from several years, making it difficult to establish consistent quality. Barbe-Nicole realized the potential of making champagne from a single exceptional crop, resulting in a product that could be sold as distinctive and superior. This invention not only distinguished her brand, but it also set a new benchmark in the industry.

Barbe-Nicole's achievements extended beyond the development of vintage champagne. One of her most notable and long-lasting inventions was the riddling table, which transformed the champagne-making process. The inclusion of sediment in the bottles, a consequence of the fermentation process, made the champagne hazy and unpleasant to customers. Traditional sediment removal procedures were time-consuming and inefficient, resulting in significant wine loss.

Barbe-Nicole, the problem solver, provided a solution to this difficulty. She invented the riddling table, a simple but clever design that allowed bottles to be placed at an angle, with the neck looking downward. By rotating the bottles on a regular basis, the sediment would gradually accumulate near the cork, making it easier to remove without losing too much wine. This method, known as remuage, became a staple of champagne manufacturing and is still employed today. The riddling table not only improved the champagne's quality and purity, but it also increased production efficiency, allowing

Barbe-Nicole to scale her operations and meet rising demand.

Her innovations went beyond the technicalities of champagne manufacturing. Barbe-Nicole was also a marketing and branding pioneer who saw the value of building a distinct identity for her champagne. She used her status as a widow, which was highly valued in French society, to promote her product as "Veuve Clicquot" — "The Widow Clicquot." This not only gave her champagne a distinctive name, but also a story that struck a chord with customers, creating an air of mystery and distinction. Another of her accomplishments was the classic yellow label, which became a symbol of quality and luxury, easily identifiable and synonymous with excellence.

Barbe-Nicole had various hurdles as she grew her business, not the least of which was the political and economic chaos caused by the Napoleonic Wars. The continental blockade, which limited trade across Europe, posed a serious threat to her activities. However, Barbe-Nicole's creativity shined through in her ability to overcome these challenges. She devised illicit trade lines and used her ties in the French government to continue exporting her champagne to Russia, one of her most valuable markets. This audacity paid off when, after Napoleon's defeat, Russian nobles embraced her champagne, notably the 1811 vintage, known as the "Comet Wine," which became a symbol of celebration and triumph.

Barbe-Nicole's growth was driven not just by expanding her market reach, but also by building an excellent business culture. She recognized that in order to maintain the high standards she had established, she needed to instill her principles in her employees. She was recognized for her hands-on attitude, frequently visiting the vineyards and collaborating closely with her winemakers to ensure that every bottle met her high standards. Her leadership approach was both firm and nurturing, cultivating an environment that valued innovation and excellence.

Barbe-Nicole continued to test the limits of her business as it grew. She pioneered innovative procedures for mixing several grape kinds, experimenting with quantities to create a champagne that was both consistent in quality and distinct in flavor. Her meticulous attention to detail extended to every step of the production process, from grape selection to maturing, ensuring that each bottle of Veuve Clicquot reflected her passion and knowledge.

Barbe-Nicole Clicquot Ponsardin's legacy lies not only in the success of her champagne business, but also in the long-term impact of her innovations on the industry. The procedures she invented, particularly the riddling table, are still utilized by champagne makers all over the world. Her approach to branding and marketing paved the way for how luxury goods are sold today, with a focus on storytelling and establishing an emotional connection with customers.

Perhaps her most important accomplishment was demonstrating that a woman could not only thrive, but flourish in a male-dominated area. Barbe-Nicole carved out a niche for herself in the economic world, utilizing her knowledge, ingenuity, and sheer willpower to construct an empire at a period when women had little influence over their own futures. She became known as the "Grande Dame of Champagne," a moniker that represented her power and esteem.

The story of Widow Clicquot exemplifies the power of ingenuity and the value of perseverance. Barbe-Nicole built Veuve Clicquot into one of the world's most prominent champagne houses, thanks to her imaginative ideas and uncompromising commitment to quality. Her legacy lives on not only in the bottles that bear her name, but also in the very fabric of the champagne business, where her ideas continue to influence how champagne is created and consumed. Veuve Clicquot is now recognized as a symbol of elegance and sophistication, a fitting tribute to the woman who defied convention and altered the course of history.

Chapter Five

The Widow's Business Acumen

Barbe-Nicole Cliquot Ponsardin, often known as the Widow Clicquot, was a woman ahead of her time. In an era when men controlled the financial world, she not only entered but succeeded in it, growing her late husband's modest wine firm into a global champagne empire. Her smart business acumen formed the foundation of this transition, as evidenced by strategic insight, unwavering resolve, and innovative thinking.

Barbe-Nicole was born into a bourgeois family in Reims, France, and was exposed to the complexities of trade from an early age. Her father, Ponce Jean Nicolas Philippe Ponsardin, was a successful textile businessman and politician who instilled in her the values of trade and negotiation. This early experience paved the way for her future undertakings, providing her with a grasp of the corporate world's complexities.

Barbe-Nicole, 27, took over the faltering family wine business after her husband, François Clicquot, died unexpectedly in 1805. At a time when widows were expected to remain in the background, she broke traditional standards by taking leadership. This brave action was the first indication of her unwavering spirit and commercial acumen. Recognizing the potential of the emerging champagne market, she was determined to carve out a space for herself and her brand.

One of the first obstacles she encountered was the aftermath of the Napoleonic Wars. The continental blockades had significantly interrupted trade routes, resulting in an economic depression. While others saw this as a deterrent, Barbe-Nicole saw it as an opportunity. She anticipated that once the conflicts were over, there would be a spike in demand for luxury items, particularly in markets that had been neglected for years. This vision prompted her to hoard her greatest vintages, ready for the impending boom. Her risk paid off when, in 1814, she was able to smuggle thousands of bottles into Russia just as the Tsar abolished trade restrictions. The Russian aristocracy, thirsty for fine champagne, embraced her product wholeheartedly, propelling the Veuve Clicquot brand to international prominence.

Barbe-Nicole's business approach revolved around innovation. Champagne production, particularly in the early nineteenth century, presented numerous problems. One of the most serious concerns was the clarity of the wine. Traditional procedures left sediment in the bottles, giving them a hazy appearance. She found a remedy after realizing that the aesthetic appeal of champagne was just as important as its flavor. She invented the riddling method in collaboration with her cellar master, Antoine de Müller. This entailed placing bottles at an angle and turning them frequently to allow sediments to settle at the neck for easy removal. This technology transformed champagne production, resulting in a clear, sparkling wine that appealed to discerning customers. The riddling procedure, which reflects her inventive spirit, is still used in champagne production today.

Barbe-Nicole's commercial skills also shown through in marketing and branding. She recognized the importance of a strong brand identity in developing client loyalty. "Veuve" means "widow" in French, and she used this moniker to her advantage. The Veuve Clicquot label, with its unique golden tint, became associated with luxury and excellence. She made her champagne synonymous with elegance, frequently sponsoring special events and ensuring that her bottles graced the tables of Europe's elite. This strategic positioning lifted her brand above competitors, establishing it as a sign of refinement.

Furthermore, Barbe-Nicole excelled at managing the difficulties of international trade. She built an extensive network of agents and distributors throughout Europe, ensuring that her champagne reached a wide range of markets. Her deep awareness of many cultures and preferences enabled her to design her items accordingly. Recognizing the Russian palate's taste for sweeter champagne, she created custom batches to meet this demand. This adaptability demonstrated her customer-centric approach, resulting in continuous development across multiple geographies.

The Widow excelled in financial management, which is generally a weakness for many organizations. She was rigorous about her bookkeeping, ensuring that expenses were justified and profits were maximized. Her willingness to reinvest profits back into the firm, whether by purchasing better vineyards or improving production procedures, demonstrated her dedication to long-term success over short-term gains. This conservative financial policy preserved the company's stability, especially during difficult economic times.

Barbe-Nicole's leadership style was a combination of toughness and empathy. She commanded respect from her colleagues, setting a good example and encouraging pride in their job. Her hands-on approach, whether in the vines or the cellar, demonstrated her commitment. She was also noted for her compassion, assuring her employees' well-being and meeting their requirements. This balance increased loyalty and inspired her team to maintain the brand's high standards.

Her capacity to adjust to shifting circumstances enhanced her business acumen. As technology improvements occurred, she was fast to incorporate them into her operations. Whether it was using new bottling techniques or exploiting evolving transportation means to broaden her reach, she remained at the forefront of innovation. This agility helped the Veuve Clicquot brand remain current and competitive.

Barbe-Nicole's triumph did not come without hurdles. The patriarchal society of nineteenth-century France frequently viewed female entrepreneurs with suspicion. She encountered opposition, both from competitors who envied her success and traditionalists who questioned her ability. However, her persistence and unshakeable faith in her mission helped her overcome these challenges. She once said, "I want my brand to rank first, from New York to Saint Petersburg." This bold assertion was more than just a statement; it reflected her persistent drive.

In summary, Widow Clicquot's financial acumen was a combination of visionary leadership, innovative thinking, and an unwavering spirit. She turned obstacles into opportunities, continually keeping ahead of the curve. Her legacy includes not only the world-renowned Veuve Clicquot brand, but also the inspiration she provides to numerous businesses, particularly women, demonstrating that drive and strategic insight can overcome societal barriers and achieve exceptional success.

Chapter Six

Veuve Clicquot's Champagne Empire

Barbe-Nicole Cliquot Ponsardin, often known as the Widow Clicquot, inherited more than just a business after her husband died unexpectedly; she inherited a legacy that needed to be shaped. Her transformation from a bereaved widow to the matriarch of one of the most prominent champagne companies is a story of resilience, inventiveness, and unwavering pursuit of greatness. Under her leadership, the Veuve Clicquot brand expanded beyond the borders of France, becoming a symbol of elegance and sophistication throughout Europe and elsewhere.

In the early nineteenth century, the champagne industry was in its infancy, and the market was far from steady. Barbe-Nicole inherited a challenging business—her late husband's champagne projects had been ambitious but not always successful. Champagne production was a complex and risky procedure, with even little errors ruining a whole batch. However, Barbe-Nicole's vision was unshakeable. She knew that in order to succeed, she needed to streamline the process, improve the quality, and establish a distinct brand for her product.

The creation of the riddling table was one of her first and most significant achievements to the champagne business. This seemingly simple breakthrough transformed the way champagne was manufactured. Traditionally, cleaning sediment from champagne bottles was labor-intensive and frequently imperfect, resulting in murky wine. The riddling table allowed bottles to be gently tilted and rotated, causing sediment to settle near the cork and be readily removed. This approach not only improved the champagne's clarity and quality, but it also increased manufacturing efficiency. The clarity of Veuve Clicquot champagne became a defining feature of its outstanding quality, distinguishing it from competitors.

Barbe-Nicole's expertise extends beyond production. She was a branding expert long before the notion became commonplace in company planning. She recognized the value of a word, and the brand 'Veuve Clicquot'—literally 'Widow Clicquot'—was meticulously constructed to convey a feeling of heritage, tradition, and exclusivity. The image of the strong, independent widow appealed to the aristocratic and expanding bourgeoisie, her main consumers. Barbe-Nicole epitomized the brand, demonstrating the characteristics of endurance and elegance. Her biography became part of the product, and each bottle of Veuve Clicquot contained a story of perseverance and perfection.

Veuve Clicquot thrived in the European market, but Barbe-Nicole aimed for even greater success. She saw the potential of the Russian market, which was virtually untouched by French champagne makers. Russia, with its immense wealth and emerging elites, was a great target for her champagne. However, selling to Russia was laden with difficulties—political unrest, logistical obstacles, and the sheer distance were formidable. Nonetheless, Barbe-Nicole's dedication was unparalleled.

Barbe-Nicole took an opportunity in 1814, as Europe emerged from the Napoleonic Wars, to secure her legacy. She discovered that Russian forces were stationed in the Champagne region, and, anticipating the conclusion of hostilities, she surreptitiously delivered her champagne ahead of her competition. This audacious initiative assured that Veuve Clicquot was the first champagne to enter the Russian market after the war. The gamble paid out spectacularly. The Russian gentry was charmed by the superb quality and crystal-clear appearance of Veuve Clicquot's champagne and embraced it enthusiastically. The Czar was believed to be a devoted fan. This breakthrough in Russia marked a watershed moment for Veuve Clicquot, elevating it to the status of a worldwide brand revered across boundaries.

The Russian market also brought with it the tale of 'comet wine.' The 1811 vintage was especially excellent, and a comet that year was interpreted as a cosmic sign of good fortune. Barbe-Nicole, ever the savvy marketer, seized on this. The 1811 vintage was dubbed the 'comet wine,' and its affiliation with this celestial event only added to its fascination and mystery. The demand for Veuve Clicquot's comet wine was insatiable, cementing the brand's place in the higher echelons of society.

As Veuve Clicquot's fame grew, so did Barbe-Nicole's business ability. She recognized that maintaining the brand's prestige needed not only outstanding product quality, but also a dedication to exclusivity. Veuve Clicquot was never about mass manufacturing; it was about producing a luxury experience, a product that was both status and taste. Each bottle made a statement, demonstrating the owner's discriminating palette.

The influence of monarchy and aristocracy was critical to the growth of Veuve Clicquot's dominion. Barbe-Nicole built contacts with key figures throughout Europe. In France, England, Austria, and, of course, Russia, Veuve Clicquot became the preferred champagne for courts and high society. The brand's link with royalty added to its attraction, making it a must-have for the most elite events and celebrations.

Barbe-Nicole's champagne was more than just a beverage; it was a symbol of grandeur and an important part of the elite's social customs.

Barbe-Nicole's success, however, was not only due to her innovative production and marketing techniques. Her unwavering attention to quality helped to distinguish Veuve Clicquot. She was thorough in every step of the production process, from grape selection to bottling. Her meticulous attention to detail meant that each bottle met the highest standards, and she was not hesitant to destroy entire batches if they did not match her stringent requirements. Her customers recognized and appreciated her commitment to quality, knowing that when they purchased Veuve Clicquot, they were getting the greatest possible product.

Maintaining the quality and status of Veuve Clicquot was no easy task, especially as the brand grew. Barbe-Nicole's leadership style was characterized by a combination of tradition and innovation. While she adhered to traditional champagne manufacturing processes, she was also open to novel approaches that could improve the product. This balance allowed Veuve Clicquot to expand while maintaining the traits that made it unique. Under her leadership, the champagne house flourished, and its products became synonymous with elegance and sophistication.

Barbe-Nicole's contribution to the champagne business cannot be emphasized. She not only established a thriving business, but she also helped define what champagne could be. Her production breakthroughs set new norms, and her branding strategy established a blueprint for luxury goods that is still used today. The Veuve Clicquot label, with its characteristic yellow-orange tint, became a symbol of elegance and refinement that was instantly recognizable around the world.

As the nineteenth century proceeded, Veuve Clicquot expanded on Barbe-Nicole's basis. Barbe-Nicole's descendants continued to operate the residence as a family business. However, it was her vision and determination that propelled it from a small, struggling business to a global empire. The brand's success in areas as disparate as Europe, Russia, and, eventually, the Americas reflects her business acumen.

The Widow Clicquot's influence lasted beyond her lifetime and shaped the development of the champagne industry. Her dedication to quality and invention inspired subsequent generations of champagne makers, and her tale served as a model for women in business. Barbe-Nicole stood out as a leader, a pioneer, and a symbol of what was possible with courage and perseverance in an era when women were frequently pushed to the outside.

Today, Veuve Clicquot is one of the world's most prominent champagne houses. Its sustained success reflects the values that Barbe-Nicole fostered in the company: excellence, creativity, and an unrelenting devotion to quality. Each bottle of Veuve Clicquot pays respect to the lady who dared to challenge convention, turned hardship into opportunity, and left a legacy that lives on nearly two centuries after her death.

The story of Widow Clicquot is more than simply a brand; it is about a lady who transformed the world. Her champagne empire was founded not just on grapes and wine, but also on vision, tenacity, and an unwavering spirit. Barbe-Nicole Clicquot Ponsardin, or the Widow Clicquot, was a true pioneer, and her story continues to inspire and enthrall those who value the better things in life.

Chapter Seven

Personal Struggles and Triumphs

Barbe-Nicole Cliquot Ponsardin, often known as the Widow Clicquot, is widely regarded as a pioneering figure in the champagne industry. Despite the brilliant prosperity and prestige of her business, her life was marked by great personal hardships and astonishing accomplishments. Her narrative is not only one of financial savvy, but also of a woman who overcame tremendous emotional and societal hurdles, emerging stronger from each struggle.

Barbe-Nicole's journey was profoundly connected with her personal life, beginning with her marriage to François Clicquot. Barbe-Nicole married François, son of a wealthy textile and wine merchant, in 1798 when she was 21 years old. The union, while founded on mutual respect and affection, was also a strategic alliance, bringing together two strong families in Reims. François, like Barbe-Nicole, had a strong enthusiasm for wine, and it was this shared interest that would serve as the foundation for their relationship. However, their marriage was not meant to last long. François' health worsened quickly, and he died in 1805, only seven years into their marriage, leaving Barbe-Nicole a widow at the age of 27.

Barbe-Nicole suffered a profound loss when François died. She was left with not only the pain of losing her boyfriend, but also the enormous responsibility of managing a struggling business. The Clicquot wine company was in debt, and the tasks ahead appeared overwhelming. In a period when widows were expected to fade into the background, Barbe-Nicole made the audacious decision to take over the company, a move almost unprecedented for a woman of her day.

Taking over the business was more than a professional decision; it was a personal mission. Barbe-Nicole was resolved to honor her husband's legacy and carry out the goal they had shared. However, the early years of her reign were beset with challenges. The champagne industry was still in its early stages, and the process of creating champagne was both intricate and labor-intensive. Barbe-Nicole encountered financial difficulties, and many advised her to sell the business and limit her losses. However, her resolve remained strong. She placed her whole fortune in the company, a daring move that may make or ruin her.

Barbe-Nicole had considerable personal hurdles, including societal expectations for women of her standing. As a widow, she was expected to live a quiet, subdued existence, relying on the men around her for support and decision-making. Barbe-Nicole chose to defy these assumptions by leading a firm in a male-dominated field. Her decision was received with skepticism and criticism from her peers, but she stood firm in her conviction.

Barbe-Nicole struggled to strike a balance between her duty as a mother and her career in the champagne industry. Clémentine, her daughter, was a young child when François died. Raising a child while also running a business was a huge responsibility, especially at a period when conventional conventions dictated that women should put family above business. Despite the pressures, Barbe-Nicole maintained a tight contact with her daughter while also directing her company to success. Her ability to juggle these responsibilities demonstrates her perseverance and determination.

During the Napoleonic Wars, Barbe-Nicole achieved one of his greatest achievements. The war devastated the European economy, and the champagne industry was no exception. With trade lines disrupted and markets falling, many wine retailers were forced to close. Despite the pandemonium, Barbe-Nicole sensed an opportunity. She took a risk by sending her champagne to Russia, which had been largely shut off from French goods due to the war. It was a dangerous maneuver because there was no guarantee the champagne would arrive at its destination or find a market for it.

Her gamble paid off. The Russians, who had been starved of luxury items during the war, were anxious to sample French champagne. The cargo was a huge success, propelling Veuve Clicquot to the ranks of the world's most prominent champagne houses. This achievement was more than just a corporate victory; it was a personal vindication for Barbe-Nicole, demonstrating that her instincts and leadership were not only sound but also visionary.

However, achievements frequently come at a cost, and Barbe-Nicole's success was not without consequences. The stress of running a thriving firm, along with the public criticism she experienced as a female entrepreneur, was enormous. Barbe-Nicole was renowned for being a highly private person, and the weight of her obligations frequently kept her secluded. Despite her public triumphs, she faced numerous internal challenges, including the loneliness that came with being a trailblazer in a world that was unprepared for women like her.

Barbe-Nicole's personal life suffered a number of setbacks in her final years. As she grew older, many of her closest friends and confidants died, leaving her to reflect on a life that was both exceptional and isolated. Despite these tragedies, she found comfort in her work and the legacy she was creating. Her connection with her daughter Clémentine continued to provide comfort, and she took great delight in preparing Clémentine to someday inherit the firm.

Barbe-Nicole's personal accomplishments lay not just in the success of her champagne, but also in how she handled the difficulties of her life. She was a lady who refused to be defined by the constraints placed on her by society. Her ambition to achieve in a male-dominated world, her ability to manage her roles as a mother and a corporate leader, and her tenacity in the face of personal and professional obstacles all demonstrate the depth of her character.

Despite the natural decline that comes with age, Barbe-Nicole remained committed in the business she had founded. She mentored the next generation of leaders, guaranteeing that the organization would thrive even after she was gone. Her influence grew beyond the champagne industry, and she became a symbol of what women might do when they refused to be limited by traditional standards.

Barbe-Nicole Cliquot Ponsardin's life exemplified the power of tenacity and vision. Her personal challenges, rather than breaking her, strengthened her resolve. Her accomplishments were not just the champagne she created, but also the barriers she broke and the legacy she left behind. The Widow Clicquot was more than a businesswoman; she was a pioneer, a mother, a leader, and a woman who, despite all difficulties, forged her own route in history.

Chapter Eight

The Widow's Later Years

Barbe-Nicole Cliquot Ponsardin, also known as Widow Clicquot, represents endurance, ingenuity, and the entrepreneurial spirit. Her later years were not merely a reflection of her exceptional accomplishments, but also a period of solidifying her legacy, a final monument to the impact she exerted in the champagne industry and beyond. These years tell the narrative of a lady who, after decades of unrivaled achievement, was able to leave an indelible impact on the globe, guaranteeing that her name would be remembered long after she died.

Barbe-Nicole approached her older years with the knowledge and elegance that comes from a life full of both victories and trials. The company she had grown from near destruction into an international powerhouse was at its peak. Veuve Clicquot had become synonymous with luxury and quality under her painstaking direction, with connoisseurs and aristocracy alike recognizing its golden label. However, the trip to this point had not been simple, and the years that followed required careful navigation to ensure that her life's work continued to prosper.

Barbe-Nicole had a number of serious issues during this period, including succession. With no male heirs to inherit the business, she had to make difficult choices about who would continue on the legacy she had established. In a society when women were rarely seen as strong business executives, Barbe-Nicole had already broken convention by operating the company herself. She needed to ensure that her chosen successors would maintain the standards she had established and continue to develop in an increasingly competitive market.

Barbe-Nicole's choice of successor was motivated by her confidence in merit and aptitude over bloodline. She had long recognized the talent of her great-nephew, Édouard Werlé, who joined the company in the early 1820s. Werlé, a visionary and astute businessman, had been crucial in expanding the brand's reach, particularly in overseas markets. His knowledge of the complexity of the champagne trade, combined with his admiration for Barbe-Nicole's methods, made him the ideal candidate to guide Veuve Clicquot into the future.

Barbe-Nicole did not simply hand over the reins and step aside. Even when she began to step back from day-to-day operations, she remained a driving force in the organization. Her advice was sought on important matters, and she was present in all aspects of the firm. This time was distinguished by a delicate balance of mentorship and progressive power transfer, ensuring that Werlé and the next generation of leaders were well prepared to take on the mantle of leadership.

As Barbe-Nicole moved into a more advising role, she made time for philanthropy and social concerns, reflecting her strong sense of community duty. She did not keep the fortune she had accumulated as a result of her economic success, but rather used it to improve the lives of others. She supported various philanthropic causes, particularly those that benefitted women and children, knowing that her own achievement was made possible by the opportunities and assistance she had received along the way.

Barbe-Nicole's later years also allowed her to reflect on her path to this point. From the young widow who took a daring risk by taking over her husband's failing business to the smart businesswoman who revolutionized the champagne industry, her life had been a series of measured risks and hard-won achievements. These insights were more than just personal musings; they were valuable lessons that she shared with people around her, ensuring that the wisdom she had received would not be lost over time.

Barbe-Nicole's influence went beyond the corporate sector. She became a symbol of what women could accomplish in a period when their roles were mostly confined to the home. Her experience motivated other women to follow their goals, to question cultural standards, and to believe in their own ability to lead and innovate. In this way, her later years were about more than just establishing her legacy in the champagne industry, but also about making a larger impact on society as a whole.

Despite their accomplishments, the following years were not without obstacles. The champagne industry was continuously changing, as new competitors emerged and market conditions shifted. Barbe-Nicole understood that the brand's sustainability rested on its capacity to adapt and evolve, just as it did under her leadership. She pushed Werlé and the team to continue pushing the boundaries, exploring new markets and experimenting with new procedures to keep Veuve Clicquot at the forefront of the industry.

Barbe-Nicole's health deteriorated naturally as she grew older. Despite her diminished physical strength, her mental acuity remained strong. She continued to interact with the company, providing insights and suggestions that were as useful as ever. Her presence served as a constant reminder of the brand's high standards of excellence, and her unwavering energy inspired everyone around her to strive for greatness in everything they did.

Barbe-Nicole's latter years were a time for reflection, not only for herself, but for everyone who had been impacted by her work and legacy. She had created something that would last beyond her lifetime, bringing joy and celebration to people all across the world. This discovery gave her a sense of relief, knowing that the risks she had taken, the battles she had waged, and the innovations she had made were all worthwhile.

Barbe-Nicole died in 1866 at the age of 89, leaving an unrivaled legacy in the wine industry. Veuve Clicquot was more than just a great corporation; it was a brand that defined the essence of champagne. The techniques she pioneered, the markets she created, and the standards she established influenced the industry for future generations.

Veuve Clicquot thrived in the years following her death, guided by Barbe-Nicole's ideals and practices. Édouard Werlé, her chosen successor, honored her memory by pushing the brand ahead and keeping it at the top of the champagne industry. The golden label, with its unmistakable yellow tint, became an enduring symbol of quality and excellence, a tribute to the woman who dared to dream large and had the fortitude to make that dream a reality.

Barbe-Nicole Clicquot Ponsardin is now known as a pioneer, innovator, and trailblazer, in addition to being a successful businesswoman. Her narrative is one of perseverance and determination, of a woman who refused to be limited by the constraints of her time, instead choosing to define herself. Her senior years were a fitting end to a wonderful journey, a time when she could look back with pride on everything she had accomplished and be confident that her legacy was secure.

Widow Clicquot's story serves as a reminder that achievement is more about the road than the destination. It is about the decisions we make, the risks we accept, and the legacy we leave behind. Barbe-Nicole's legacy was one of quality, innovation, and an unwavering pursuit of greatness—one that continues to inspire and impact people today.

Chapter Nine

The Brand After the Widow

Barbe-Nicole Ponsardin, also known as Widow Clicquot, passed away, but the narrative of Veuve Clicquot continued. In reality, her legacy as the driving force behind one of the world's most renowned champagne houses grew stronger as the business evolved long after her death. The foundation she laid was so strong that the Veuve Clicquot brand became synonymous with elegance, innovation, and perfection in the champagne industry. Veuve Clicquot's trajectory following the Widow's Era demonstrates the lasting impact of her vision, drive, and financial skill.

Following Madame Clicquot's death in 1866, the company faced the difficulty of retaining the respect and image she had worked so hard to establish. Her successors understood that they were not just running a business; they were caretakers of a legacy. The brand had become legendary, thanks to its distinctive yellow label and high quality standards, both of which consumers considered non-negotiable. Any divergence from these standards could harm the brand's reputation, which cannot be risked in an increasingly competitive market.

One of the most noteworthy changes in the post-Widow Clicquot era was the increased emphasis on innovation. While Barbe-Nicole pioneered the essential riddling procedure, which increased the clarity and quality of champagne, her successors did not rest on their laurels. They recognized that in the luxury goods market, innovation is a constant endeavor rather than a one-time triumph. This commitment to continuous improvement helped Veuve Clicquot remain at the forefront of the champagne business. Whether it was upgrading production procedures, flavor profiles, or packaging, the company continued to innovate in ways that honored Madame Clicquot's tradition while also appealing to consumers' shifting tastes and preferences.

Another important component of the brand's evolution was its entry into new markets. During Barbe-Nicole's lifetime, Veuve Clicquot had already made considerable inroads into the Russian market, where the champagne became popular among the Russian aristocracy. Following her death, the brand's international reach grew even further. The company's objective was to preserve the quality and distinction associated with Veuve Clicquot across multiple markets. This was especially crucial as the brand entered countries where consumers were unfamiliar with champagne or faced stiff competition from other established brands.

The expansion was not only geographical, but it also included product diversification. While Veuve Clicquot was recognized for its brut champagne, the company began to create other kinds that appealed to a variety of tastes. This included the introduction of rosé champagne, which immediately became popular. The introduction of these additional items was carefully planned to compliment rather than diminish the brand's character. Every new product had to fulfill Madame Clicquot's strict standards, and this devotion to quality served to solidify the brand's position as a champagne industry leader.

Veuve Clicquot's capacity to adapt to shifting market conditions was also critical to the company's ongoing success. Consumer behavior changes and shifts affect the champagne business, as they do many others. For example, during economic downturns, luxury items frequently witness a drop in sales as buyers tighten their belts. However, Veuve Clicquot was able to overcome these obstacles by emphasizing that its champagne was more than just a product, but also an experience, a symbol of celebration, and an expression of exquisite taste. This approach enabled the company to maintain its attractiveness throughout difficult economic times.

The importance of marketing in the post-Widow Clicquot era cannot be overstated. The brand's unique yellow label was an effective marketing tool, readily recognisable and linked with quality and elegance. This branding was about more than simply the hue; it was also about what it symbolized. The yellow label came to represent Madame Clicquot's daring and inventive character. The company's marketing methods were aimed to evoke the elegance, sophistication, and exclusivity that defined the Veuve Clicquot brand. These methods helped maintain the brand current and appealing to succeeding generations of consumers.

Veuve Clicquot's tale following the Widow's death also concerns the company's ability to maintain its independence and distinct identity in an industry that has seen tremendous consolidation. In 1987, Veuve Clicquot joined the Louis Vuitton Moët Hennessy (LVMH) group, a premium corporation that owns other notable brands. While joining a larger company may have diluted the brand's character, Veuve Clicquot has managed to maintain its uniqueness inside the LVMH portfolio. The corporation maintained a high level of autonomy, ensuring that Madame Clicquot's traditions and principles were upheld. This autonomy enabled Veuve Clicquot to stay true to its beginnings while simultaneously leveraging the resources and experience of a larger corporate body.

The globalization of the Veuve Clicquot brand was another key development following the Widow's era. The brand's champagne started to reach far-flung regions like North America, Asia, and beyond. This global reach was achieved not alone through distribution, but also through a concentrated effort to establish the brand's image in these new areas. Veuve Clicquot became a global icon of elegance and sophistication, with the champagne served at high-profile events, appearing in films and television shows, and relished by celebrities and royalty. The brand's affiliation with high society and exclusivity helped to solidify its status as one of the world's top champagne houses.

Widow Clicquot's effect on the champagne business extended beyond the Veuve Clicquot name. Other champagne houses and premium brands have studied and replicated her manufacturing advances, marketing approaches, and business tactics. Madame Clicquot's legacy is visible in the evolution of the champagne industry, which has placed a premium on quality, branding, and innovation as a result of her pioneering efforts. Her narrative continues to inspire entrepreneurs and business executives, particularly women, who see her as a role model for achieving success through vision, determination, and hard work.

In the current period, Veuve Clicquot has built on this legacy by engaging with contemporary audiences in novel and imaginative ways. To reach a younger, more diversified audience, the company has turned to digital marketing, social media, and experiential events. These initiatives have succeeded in exposing the brand to new generations of customers while preserving the core values and heritage that distinguish Veuve Clicquot. The brand's capacity to evolve while remaining true to its origins is critical to its long-term success.

Veuve Clicquot's story following the Widow's death is one of careful stewardship, purposeful innovation, and a strong regard for tradition. The brand's sustained success demonstrates the enduring legacy of Madame Clicquot's vision and the dedication of those who have followed in her footsteps. Today, Veuve Clicquot is more than simply champagne; it is a symbol of excellence, a celebration of life, and a monument to a great lady who altered the course of history. The true story of Widow Clicquot, the champagne woman, lives on in every bottle that bears her name, a legacy that sparkles as brightly as the champagne she worked so hard to perfect.

Chapter Ten

The Lasting Impact of Widow Clicquot

Barbe-Nicole Cliquot Ponsardin, often known as the Widow Clicquot, has made an unmistakable imprint on the champagne business that continues to this day. Her life exemplified endurance, inventiveness, and an unwavering resolve to achieve in an era when the world was not yet ready to accept a woman as a corporate leader. Her narrative, as told in *Widow Clicquot: The True narrative of the Champagne Woman*, is not only one of personal achievement, but also of a lasting legacy that has influenced the champagne business and others.

Barbe-Nicole's adventure began under the shadow of the French Revolution, a turbulent period during which many fortunes rose and fell. Born into an affluent family, she married François Clicquot, a wine enthusiast. But when François died unexpectedly, Barbe-Nicole found herself widowed at the age of 27, with a small daughter to care for and a fledgling wine business to manage. In an era when women were expected to remain at home, her choice to take over her husband's business was nothing short of revolutionary.

Widow Clicquot's impact on the champagne business was immediate and significant. She inherited a company that was failing to gain traction in a highly competitive field, yet she saw opportunity where others saw disaster. Her first significant breakthrough was the production of the first known vintage champagne in 1810.

This was a risky move because champagne was not traditionally connected with vintages. Barbe-Nicole recognized that by developing a wine that could be aged and enhanced over time, she might create a product that would distinguish itself from the competition. This choice paved the way for Veuve Clicquot to become synonymous with quality and luxury.

Her subsequent innovation, however, truly distinguished her. Barbe-Nicole is credited with inventing the riddling table, which enabled her to make crystal-clear champagne by efficiently removing sediment from the bottles. This procedure, called "remuage," transformed the champagne-making process and is still employed today. The riddling table not only increased the quality of her champagne, but it also allowed her to increase production, allowing Veuve Clicquot to satisfy rising demand for its product.

Widow Clicquot's success was not solely due to her technological inventions; she was also a skilled marketer. She recognized the value of branding and was among the first to use a label to differentiate her bottles from those of her competitors. Veuve Clicquot's distinctive yellow label became a sign of excellence and sophistication, contributing to the brand's reputation among consumers. She also saw the value of overseas markets and moved quickly to grow her firm beyond France. Her champagne gained popularity in Russia, where it was dubbed "Comet Wine" because to its relationship with the Great Comet of 1811. This early foray into global marketing served to establish Veuve

Clicquot as one of the world's premier champagne houses.

Barbe-Nicole's influence went beyond the corporate sector. She was a pioneer in a traditionally male-dominated field, demonstrating that women could excel at the highest echelons of business. Her leadership style was characterized by determination, inventiveness, and pragmatism. She was not afraid to take risks, but she also knew when to exercise caution. Her success spurred other women to pursue their own entrepreneurial goals, breaking established gender stereotypes at the time.

The Veuve Clicquot brand's ongoing success reflects Widow Clicquot's legacy. Veuve

Clicquot is still one of the most prominent champagne brands more than two centuries after she took over the firm. Barbe-Nicole's leadership laid the groundwork for the company's devotion to quality and innovation. Today, Veuve Clicquot continues to push the boundaries of champagne production, with an emphasis on sustainability and innovation that would have made its creator pleased.

The most crucial component of Barbe-Nicole's legacy, however, is her ability to shift people's perceptions of what women could achieve in business. She developed an empire that has lasted for generations, despite the fact that women were mostly barred from the realm of commerce. Her narrative serves as a reminder that with vision, determination, and a willingness to challenge convention, greatness can be achieved, no matter what hurdles arise.

In popular culture, Widow Clicquot has come to represent fortitude and resilience. Her narrative has been told in a number of novels, documentaries, and films, each focusing on a different aspect of her life and legacy. She is frequently presented as a woman ahead of her time, refusing to be limited by societal standards and forging a path for others to follow. Her name has become synonymous with elegance and sophistication, but it is her persistence and vision that actually distinguishes her.

Widow Clicquot has also had an impact on the champagne industry as a whole. Her production and marketing techniques helped boost champagne from a regional specialty to a global premium product. She was instrumental in developing champagne's reputation as a drink linked with celebration and grandeur, which still exists today. The processes she created and the standards she established continue to guide the industry, ensuring champagne's status as one of the world's most prestigious beverages.

Furthermore, Barbe-Nicole's influence goes beyond the realm of champagne. She is a source of inspiration for businesses, particularly women, who regard her tale as an example of resilience and accomplishment. Her life exemplifies the power of invention and the value of sticking to one's vision in the face of insurmountable obstacles. Her ability to manage the responsibilities of company with her personal life teaches vital lessons for current leaders, especially in an era when work-life balance is widely regarded as a critical component of success.

The story of Widow Clicquot is about empowerment and transformation, not just business success. Her actions challenged the status quo and changed what women might achieve at the time. Her legacy includes not only the champagne that carries her name, but also the innumerable women who have followed in her footsteps, inspired by her example to pursue their own goals and overcome the obstacles in their path.

As we consider Widow Clicquot's long-term impact, it becomes evident that her contributions to the champagne business were only one aspect of her tale. She was a visionary leader who saw the potential of innovation and the importance of adhering to one's ideals. Her ability to manage the challenges of her period and create a brand that has persisted for centuries demonstrates her exceptional talent and determination. Today, when we raise a glass of Veuve Clicquot in celebration, we do it not only to commemorate the champagne, but also to the woman who made it possible. Barbe-Nicole Clicquot Ponsardin, aka the Widow Clicquot, is a lasting emblem of greatness, inspiration, and the transformational power of one woman's vision.